KITTENS

Caring for
Your Pet

Hannelore Grimm

Enslow Publishers, Inc.
40 Industrial Road
Box 398
Berkeley Heights, NJ 07922
USA

http://www.enslow.com

Contents

1

KITTENS

Other titles in the series

Keeping and Caring for Your Pet

Fish: Keeping and Caring for Your Pet
Library Edition ISBN 978-0-7660-4185-1
Paperback ISBN 978-1-4644-0301-9

Guinea Pigs: Keeping and Caring for Your Pet
Library Edition ISBN 978-0-7660-4184-4
Paperback ISBN 978-1-4644-0299-9

Puppies: Keeping and Caring for Your Pet
Library Edition ISBN 978-0-7660-4187-5
Paperback ISBN 978-1-4644-0305-7

Rabbits: Keeping and Caring for Your Pet
Library Edition ISBN 978-0-7660-4183-7
Paperback ISBN 978-1-4644-0297-5

1

Choosing and Bringing Home a Kitten

A Good Start
Building Trust From Day One

A kitten has the ability to instantly capture a person's heart. He charms everyone he meets, even those who are skeptical at first. Once a person has seen the little whirlwind racing around the house and cuddled him on her lap, she will be sold. Who could possibly resist?

Carefree and Sassy

Where is he? Is he asleep? Has he eaten? The new kitten is so cute and vulnerable, he brings out the nurturing side in everyone. He also seems to get away with quite a bit of mischief—certainly a lot more than his mother would have tolerated. Kittens expect rules and restrictions from you, so training him early on is the best way to deal with any bad behavior.

House cats do not like to be alone. If you are short on time, get your cat a playmate.

→ Cat or Smaller Pet?

In contrast to a smaller pet, such as a hamster or guinea pig, a cat is free to roam around the house; jump on chairs, tables, and cabinets; and has access to anything that is not locked away. It does take some effort to housebreak your cat. But what makes cats so appealing is the way they approach you for a cuddle and show their appreciation with a loud purr.

Bad Habits

Certain habits that have not been immediately forbidden can lead to a badly behaved adult cat. Think of the pleasure your kitten gets from pouncing on hands and feet. Tiny kitten claws do not hurt, but adult cat claws can cause a lot of damage. The same goes for clawing the sofa or curtains, or jumping onto the kitchen counter or dining room table. These are perfectly natural cat behaviors that could prove destructive to your property. With some patience and time, you can control them. Your little kitten must learn boundaries right from the start. He may still be young, but by twelve weeks of age, he will have developed his own personality with unique traits.

Two Cats Are Better Than One

Cats are natural loners, but they are also very adaptable creatures. Two cats that grow up together can become great friends. Even when you are away, your cats would always have someone to play with, snuggle with, and talk to!

Test

Are You Ready for a Cat?

Ask yourself the following questions and answer them honestly with a simple yes or no.

- ☐ Am I prepared to care for my cat every day for the rest of his life (12–18 years)?

- ☐ Is my home suitable for a cat?

- ☐ Can I deal with his shedding and using the sofa as a scratching post?

- ☐ Do I have enough money for daily costs, as well as vet bills?

- ☐ Do I have enough time to care for a kitten, pet him, and play with him?

- ☐ Is every family member allergy-free?

- ☐ Is there someone who could look after my cat if I went on vacation?

- ☐ Will he simply be allowed to be a cat? He will not make a suitable substitute for a dog or child!

Did you answer every question with a "yes"? Great! Then you are ready to get a kitten!

Your Role: Mother Cat

You, as the owner and main caretaker, will play the role of the cat's mother (even if you are a boy because kittens are always cared for by their mothers, not their fathers). All other family members, including other children, dogs, or other cats, are like siblings or relatives who have to get along with one another.

Once your cat has moved in, you will need to take on some duties, such as feeding and cleaning the litter box.

Ready for a Cat?
Your New Kitten

Simply put, cats do not like to spend too much time alone. An entire day on her own can feel like forever to a cat. Therefore, it is not a good idea to leave your cat alone in the house for more than eight hours. Even if she does not seem as lonely as a dog might seem, if she has to spend every day alone, she might eventually show signs of being upset; for example, she may stop washing herself.

A Pair of Cats?

Choose your favorite two kittens out of the same litter. Get them neutered or spayed early on, if one is female and one is male, so that you do not end up with any unwanted kittens. Two cats are not really much more work than one, but they will help balance each other out and keep themselves amused when they are alone in the house. And, of course, two cats mean twice the cuddles. Take time to think it over. Whether you decide to have one or more cats, each situation has its advantages and disadvantages.

Scientifically Proven

If you are still not convinced about getting a second cat then consider this: it has been scientifically proven that two cat companions will live longer than one lonely cat because they will play and exercise more together and generally feel happier.

A Second Cat a Few Years Later?

It is best to introduce a new cat during the first six months of your kitten's life. If you have an adult cat, then the second cat should be around three to four months of age. It is less problematic this way, especially if the new cat is a different gender. The older cat will train the younger cat.

> → **Think It Over**
> *Despite popular belief, cats do not need to go outside to be happy. What they really need is their own little community. If you have a choice, then the best solution is to get two kittens to keep each other company.*

The Right Scent

So that both cats have the "right scent" from the start, spray your hands with perfume or aftershave and then stroke both cats.

Male or Female?

If you want to keep only one cat, then the gender should not really be an issue. There are no serious differences in the behavior of either gender. Both females and males are loving, intelligent, and playful. Males tend to be slightly larger. Both genders should be neutered or spayed, however, the neutering of males is a more straightforward procedure.

Cats have more fun together, especially if your cats are left alone in the house all day.

Pets Allowed?

If you live in a house your parents own and you have their permission, then you do not need to worry. But you may have problems keeping pets if you live in an apartment or rented house. You need permission from the landlord to keep a cat. A ban on pets may already have been stated in the rental agreement. In this case, the landlord may be prepared to bend the rules. If a cat disturbs the household in an unreasonable manner, the landlord may decide to forbid cats.

Mixed Breed or Pedigree?

It is false to say that a pedigree cat is not as healthy as a mixed-breed cat. In fact, a pedigree cat is wormed from birth, whereas a mixed-breed cat may not

Good to Know for Tenants   Tip

Landlords may give permission to keep cats in the rental agreement. What they often do not realize is, they need a very good reason to decide to dishonor this agreement. This gives the tenant a good chance to argue his or her case for keeping the cat. A landlord will rarely be able to forbid a "reasonable number" of clean house cats (no more than two), in most cases.

be taken to the vet's office to be wormed until he is two or three months old. But some breeds are more likely than others to have certain health problems. Take the time to look at lots of cats before you make a decision. Be critical and use common sense.

If you decide to get a kitten, he will need to be wormed and vaccinated.

Suitable for All
House Cats

The majority of cats are bred from the domestic cat family. They come in all colors and patterns, but gray tabby is the most common coat. A tabby cat's eyes are almost always green. The short fur is easy to groom and thanks to their innate cleanliness, most cats take very good care of themselves.

Call of the Wild

The offspring of free-roaming cats, which are the majority of cats, will soon show a great desire for freedom, and they will only stay inside at all times if they are made to do so.

Where to Get a House Cat?

It should not be too difficult to acquire a cat. Kittens can usually be bought from a breeder. You could also get a kitten from an animal shelter for a small donation, which will then go toward helping other cats in the shelter; the fee would help pay for food or vet bills, for example. Or perhaps a cat in your neighborhood has had a litter of kittens. Whether from animal shelters or private means, there is always a way to find your ideal kitten. Kittens from a well-run animal shelter are usually vaccinated and examined by a vet for a nominal fee or small donation. You can ask your vet to recommend a good animal shelter.

If a cat has experienced the "call of the wild," it may be difficult for him to adjust to a life indoors.

Homebody   *Tip*

If a house cat has not previously experienced the freedom of the great outdoors, then he should adjust quite quickly to the life of an indoor cat.

At Least Eight Weeks Old

Many people selling or giving away kittens want them to find good homes as soon as possible. However, the kitten should be at least eight weeks old, but preferably ten to twelve weeks old, so that he has had a chance to develop his social skills and has been properly weaned from his mother. Any necessary veterinary care, especially vaccinations, are then the owner's responsibility.

How About a Pedigree Cat?

If you wish to keep your cat indoors, you may consider getting a pedigree cat as a future housemate. A healthy, wormed, vaccinated pedigree cat can cost hundreds of dollars and should be bought from a reputable breeder who provides a receipt of purchase and pedigree papers.

Everyday Costs

You may spend about $35 per month for good quality food and litter. Then there are the annual checkups and vaccinations against feline distemper, cat flu, leukemia, and rabies. So you will need to set aside about $30 to $50 per month for vet costs, not including visits due to illness or injury. How much you spend depends on the brands of food and litter, your cat's health, and how much the vet charges.

Quiet or Frisky?

Whether you choose the quietest or the friskiest kitten from the litter is completely up to you. Try to choose the kitten that best suits you and fits in with your way of life. Take time to play with and observe each individual kitten. Proceed with caution because once you have made your purchase, there is no going back. Your new friend could be with you for many years to come.

Do you want a quiet or frisky kitten? It is completely up to your own individual preferences. Choose the kitten which best suits you.

Health Checklist

- [ ] The abdomen should not be swollen, hard, or tense.
- [ ] The anus should be clean and should not smell.
- [ ] The eyes should be clear, and the third eyelid, called the nictitating membrane, should not be visible.
- [ ] The gums should be pink and the teeth white with no deformities (overbite or underbite).
- [ ] The ears should be clean and free of any black mucus (this is an indication of ear mites).
- [ ] The coat should be thick, soft, shiny, and clean, without any knots or tangles.
- [ ] The fur should not have any bald patches.
- [ ] The skin should be free from rashes and inflammation.
- [ ] The fur should not contain any parasites. Small black specks are caused by fleas and could indicate an infestation.

Persian, British Shorthair, and Siamese

Whether you would like a British shorthair or Persian longhair, the most popular breeds are well established. Some are very people-orientated and have peaceful characters. The liveliest cat of all is the Siamese cat.

Persian

Persians are a relatively old breed and have been popular for more than a century. Out of all the cat breeds, they have the longest fur and the shortest noses. They used to be called Angoras, which is a term that is now only used to describe the Turkish Angora. The beautiful coat of a Persian cat is not easy to keep clean and daily grooming is required. The kitten will need to become accustomed to grooming very early on.

The exotic shorthair is the short-haired version of the Persian. It comes in all the colors the Persian comes in but is easier to groom.

Himalayans

Himalayans belong to the Persian family and used to be known as Khmer cats. In Europe, they are also called colorpoint Persians. They have the body type and long-haired coat of the Persian. But they are also part Siamese, as shown by their beautiful blue eyes and their fur color, which is lighter on the body with darker-colored markings on the face, ears, legs, and tail. They are available in the same colors as Siamese cats.

Chinchilla

Some see chinchillas as a separate breed. However, in reality, these also belong to the Persian family. The white fur has black tips at the end, which gives it a kind of "powdered" effect. If the black tips are larger, then the cats are called silver-shaded.

Left: Persian cats are quiet and cuddly, but their long fur is high maintenance.

Right: This British shorthair has a blue-gray and cream coat.

British Shorthair (BSH)

The blue British shorthair (British blue) is probably the best-known representative of this breed. The British shorthair comes in many colors, not just in the well-known blue-gray. One of the latest variations to the breed is the British colorpoint shorthair that is crossed with Siamese. The overall appearance of this breed is a short nose, large amber-colored eyes, and a large sturdy body. The thick, glossy, short fur feels like velvet. These beautiful creatures have a quiet, easygoing nature, although they can sometimes be quite stubborn. It is much less work to care for this breed than, for example, a Persian. Nevertheless, the loose fur will need to be combed out once a week or so.

Siamese and Oriental Shorthair

Oriental cats are recognized by their extremely slender and elongated bodies, wedge-shaped heads, and large ears. The best-known breed is the Siamese. Siamese cats with medium-length fur are also bred under the name of Balinese. Without the typical Siamese features—blue eyes and the pointed coat pattern—these cats are known as Oriental shorthair or Javanese, if their coat is of medium length. Their fiery temperament is in contrast to their sleek, elegant appearance. They are very talkative, affectionate, and sociable cats.

→ A Cat as a Gift?

A living animal can be the nicest gift of all, if the recipient has always wanted one and all necessary preparations have been made. An animal will need your love and affection for many years to come.

Always remember, a cat or other animal should not be a surprise gift!

Unfortunately, out of thoughtlessness (or for whatever reason), some people still buy a pet like they would a computer game as a birthday or holiday gift. An animal is not a toy you can put in a corner after the holidays are over, and then bring out when you need something to play with.

Siamese

Siamese cats have dazzling, deep blue, almond-shaped eyes. The four main colors are seal point, chocolate point, blue point, and lilac point. Until the mid-1950s, they were slightly sturdier, but the current breed has an extremely streamlined figure. The Siamese is a real chatterbox and certainly has plenty to say to his owner!

The Siamese cat is characterized by his blue eyes, cream-colored fur, and dark-colored points—the ears, tail, feet, and "mask" on the face.

Maine Coon and Other Breeds

Semi-long-haired cats require significantly less maintenance than Persians. These impressive cats have a medium-length coat, and in contrast to Persians, do not have a thick undercoat and therefore the coat is less prone to knotting. In summer, the coat is significantly shorter and brighter than in winter. Nevertheless, these impressive cats still need to be groomed, especially during the shedding season.

Turkish Angoras pick out one favorite family member. These cats are sociable, child friendly, and very vocal. They also enjoy jumping.

Maine Coon

The Maine coon is one of the largest and most primitive breed of cats. It originated in Maine, and its appearance has remained almost unchanged for more than one hundred years. The Maine coon comes in many different colors. This cat is characterized by her affectionate nature and gentle voice. Maine coons make pleasant housemates.

Norwegian Forest Cat

The Norwegian forest cat is a big, strong, muscular semi-long-haired cat, but she is not quite as big as the Maine coon. Her head is triangular, with a long nose and flat side profile. The ears are large and pointed. The exterior appearance of this cat is very natural, wild, and strong. Her character is lively but gentle, intelligent, affectionate, and friendly.

Turkish Angora

The Turkish Angora is also just known as the Angora or the Turkish cat. It is a semi-long-haired cat with a slim body. This breed is not related to the Turkish Van, which only comes in a particular coat pattern: white with colored patches on the head and tail. Van cats are very intelligent and, unlike other cats, enjoy the water.

Older Is Better

Pedigree cats should not go to new owners until they are twelve weeks old because the kittens must first be wormed and vaccinated. The initial vaccination will be given between the ages of seven to eight weeks. The booster vaccination comes three weeks later. By then, the kittens will be at least eleven weeks old. The breeder will keep the cat for one more week to check she has not had an adverse reaction to the vaccine.

These two ragdoll kittens are already very curious.

Birman

The Birman is a semi-long-haired cat with a moderately long body and relatively short but strong legs with rounded paws. The coat pattern is similar to the Siamese, and the eyes are blue. The special feature of this breed are its four white paws. The Birman is lively, sociable, and very affectionate. These cats like cuddles and need a lot of attention.

Ragdoll

The loving and friendly ragdolls become tenderly attached to their owners and never want to be alone. They follow people around, love to play, and are always eager to join in on the action. Their body shape and coat is similar to that of a Birman cat. The ragdoll originates from the United States and there are four coat patterns: colorpoint, bicolor, mitted, and van. The colorpoint ragdoll has typical Siamese markings—a darker nose, ears, tail, and paws. The bicolor ragdoll has white paws, a white belly and chest, and a characteristic white upside-down "V" on the face. Mitted ragdolls look like colorpoints but have white paws, a white chin, a white stripe on the belly, and sometimes, a white patch on the forehead and nose. A van-patterned ragdoll has a white body with color on the top of the head, ears, and tail. All ragdolls have blue eyes.

> ### → *Where to Buy a Pedigree Kitten*
> *If you are looking for a pedigree cat, your best bet is to get one from a reputable breeder. The breeder will have all the paperwork proving that your cat is a purebred. Some breeders advertise in newspapers or magazines such as* Cat Fancy, *or they advertise at cat associations and clubs. Perhaps the best-known cat organization in the United States is the Cat Fanciers' Association. Each breed of cat has its own organization as well.*

Rare and Exotic
Burmese, Ocicat, and More

Russian Blue

A charming, quiet, but strong-willed creature, the Russian blue is particularly drawn to an even-tempered person with a quiet voice. This cat is not fond of noise. She has an elongated, slender body and a short, wedge-shaped head with a heart-shaped face and widely spaced, almond-shaped eyes in a lively shade of green. Her most characteristic feature is her unique double-layered, blue-gray fur.

Burmese

The Burmese is a medium-sized cat with smooth, fine, and very short hair. She is very friendly, graceful, energetic, and affectionate toward humans. These cats are described as "doglike" because of their devotion to their favorite people.

Abyssinian

One of the oldest cat breeds is the Abyssinian. This breed embodies the beautiful ideal of the elegant ancient Egyptian cat goddess Bast. An Abyssinian's fur is dense, short, and fine. The fur is ticked, which means individual hairs have bands of dark and light colors, similar to the pattern found on the coats of wild rabbits. This is why Abyssinians used to be referred to as "hare-cats." In a standard Abyssinian, each hair is light at the root, brown-orange (ruddy) in the middle, and black at the tip.

There are also red, blue, and fawn variations. This cat has a muscular, medium-sized slim body. The Abyssinian is a very tame and cuddly cat that is also brave. She is not a nervous cat at all and rarely makes use of her gentle voice. Most Abyssinians are very athletic. All are enthusiastic climbers, and many of them can open doors. They are very lively cats with an especially strong hunting instinct, so you will need plenty of space!

Somali

The Somali cat is basically a long-haired Abyssinian. All features belonging to the two breeds are identical, except for the longer fur. Because of her long coat, she is often compared to a lynx or to a fox if her fur is red in color.

Image above: The Egyptian Mau, here in silver, is the cat featured in ancient Egyptian artwork.

Right: The Somali cat is the long-haired version of the Abyssinian.

Rex Cats

Rex cats have wavy or curly fur. The unusual fur texture was a natural mutation. The different types are the Devon rex, Cornish rex, German rex, and Selkirk rex. They are available in several color variations and the Selkirk rex is even available with different coat lengths. The appearance of this cat takes some getting used to, but once you get to know one of these charming and extremely affectionate cats, you cannot help but fall in love.

Ocicat and Egyptian Mau

The Ocicat and Egyptian Mau breeds are short-haired breeds. Both cats have strong spotted patterns and can be very temperamental. However, they do make good family pets.

Chartreux

The real Chartreux almost ceased to exist altogether. This breed was crossed with the blue British shorthair and only a few purebred cats from French lineage escaped this mix. Just as the British shorthair is quite sturdy, so is the Chartreux. This is a rather "square-shaped" cat and only available in blue.

The Ocicat has a beautiful spotted coat and a spirited temperament.

Tip

Breeding Cats

If you want to breed your cat, it is better to choose a female kitten. At the onset of sexual maturity, male cats will scent-mark your home with a very unpleasant odor. If you have no intention of breeding your cat, it is a good idea to have him or her neutered or spayed by six months of age.

Preparing your home for the arrival of your new kitten can be great fun. You can get everything you need from a pet supply store or on the Internet and have it delivered to the house. You can find an overview of what your cat will need on pages 30 and 31.

The Scratching Post

Sleep, Climb, Sharpen Claws

To protect your furniture, you should get your kitten used to a scratching post, scratching board, or cat tree as soon as possible. The advantage of a scratching tree is that not only can she manicure her claws, but she can also exercise her muscles by climbing the tree, and she has a place to sleep at the top. Many scratching posts and boards come with catnip to entice your cat to use it. You can also buy catnip spray. If you scratch the post as your cat watches, he will usually start scratching it, too.

Stability

The most important thing for a cat tree is stability. If your cat topples over her scratching post, she will never use it again! Do not put it away in the corner. A cat will not scratch the inside of a closet, for example. She prefers to scratch in obvious places that are easy to access, such as the edge of the sofa in the living room, so give her a cat tree in its place.

Cat Bed

Sleeping Place

Many cat books will tell you that your kitten needs a cat bed to sleep in. There is no guarantee that your cat will sleep in the bed you have bought for her! Cats always find their own places to sleep. A simple cardboard box with a cushion inside is a good place to start. The advantage of a box is that if your cat has an accident, you can just get her a new box, which can be then swapped for a bigger one as your cat grows.

Somewhere Up High

My cats will very rarely sleep on the floor. They prefer to sleep somewhere up high. A hammock (for example, one attached to the scratching post) is ideal and ensures a small kitten will not fall from a high place. Cats love warm, draft-free areas, so place your cat's bed in a cozy area. Whether she actually chooses to sleep there is another matter!

Bedtime Buddies

Most cats will probably choose your bed as their place to camp out. As long as you do not mind this, then it is not a problem. If you do not want company, then there is only one solution—keep the door shut. After a week or two, the kitten should learn to accept this house rule.

Your cat will need a scratching post, somewhere to sleep, food and water bowls, and a litter box.

Cats are marathon sleepers.

The Feeding Area
Cats Need Three Bowls

It is recommended that you use two separate bowls for wet and dry food, which should be shallow, heavy, and easy to clean. Use a large, sturdy bowl for water. Avoid porous material such as plastic. Bacteria can grow in the tiny scratches and holes that may form. Use stainless steel, glass, or ceramic instead. The food area should be easy to clean and not too small, as cats tend to take a chunk of food from their bowl and put it on the floor somewhere . . . hopefully not too far from the food bowl!

The Litter Box
When Nature Calls

By nature, cats are clean animals. Cat litter, a litter box, and a scoop are necessary items. Since cats like to urinate and defecate in two different areas, it would be a good idea to have two litter boxes.

Cat Litter

Fill up the litter box with at least two inches of cat litter so that your cat can bury her business without leaving a trace. Stores offer different types of litter—clay, clumping, crystals, recycled paper pellets, corn, and wheat—so you can find one to suit your cat. Do not move the litter box around because your cat is a creature of habit and always likes to go in the same place. This is usually the reason why she may decide to go outside of her litter box. The litter box should be emptied and cleaned at least once a week.

The Toilet Area

Cats can be very shy about going to the bathroom and do not like being watched. Therefore, you should put the litter box in a quiet corner and preferably somewhere the dog cannot reach. It is important that your cat can reach this space at any time she needs to.

Make sure your kitten always has access to water, a bowl of dry or wet food, and a litter box. Keep the food and water away from the litter box.

A Place in the Sun

Cats can spend hours at the window, just sitting and watching the world go by. If you want to give your indoor cat the pleasure of sitting by an open window, you could cover the window with wire mesh or a fly screen. Fresh air is good for cats. Make sure you reserve her place on the windowsill and keep it free of clutter.

Caution: Deadly Trap!

Hopper windows or bottom hung windows are fatal traps. If the cat climbs up to the gap at the top and his back legs slip on the glass frame, he could get his neck or stomach trapped in the gap. You can prevent this by using a tilting window protection device, which stops the frame from slipping down and your cat from getting trapped.

Balcony Nets

If you have a balcony, it is only natural you would want to share this with your cat. Inevitably, though, your cat will want to satisfy his curiosity by climbing on the railings and the hunting instinct could kick in, causing him to chase after a bird or butterfly and then fall. Do not assume your cat will not jump—he may get distracted. Depending on where he lands and how far he falls, this jump could be fatal or cause him serious injury. If possible, you will need to make your balcony safe by using a net. Some companies specialize in balcony nets for this purpose. It is relatively easy to put up the net using screws and cable clamps, thus making your balcony a safe place for your cat.

The Cat-Proof Yard

Perhaps you are lucky enough to have your own backyard and want to share this with your cat. In that case, you should cat-proof your yard. But you still need to be aware of the risks of letting him run around and also keep on good terms with the rest of the neighborhood in case he escapes.

Once your cat has a taste of freedom, it will be very hard to keep her inside the house.

→ *Outdoors or Indoors?*

Stay inside and daydream or go outside and run around? Deciding whether or not to let your cat out is something you need to think over. It all depends on your own personal wishes as well as your new cat's previous domestic situation. Even a twelve-week-old kitten may have already been accustomed to freedom, for example, if he was born on a farm.

Fencing

The easiest way to cat-proof your yard is to use slim poles and a wire-mesh fence. You could use mosquito or bird nets, but you can also buy special cat nets. Hammer the poles five feet apart into the ground and attach the net so it is taut. The net should be about six and a half feet high. About twenty inches from the bottom, attach chicken wire and make sure it is buried about four inches into the ground as some cats can develop the digging skills of a mole! When the cat attempts to climb the net, she will realize it is not very supportive and will soon get bored trying to climb it.

Why Are So Many Cats Allowed to Go Outside?

Although there are many good arguments for keeping a cat indoors, most cats will try to escape outside if this is somehow possible. The reason why most manage it is simple: cats are extremely determined creatures and will show great perseverance when they want something. They love to be outside, roaming freely and independently and chasing mice and other small prey.

What Are the Arguments Against Outdoor Cats?

Stray cats do not live long. Many are run over by cars or killed by predators. Cats are scavengers and can sometimes be poisoned, for example, from water barrels. A cat may be stolen, harmed in a cat fight, hurt by a person, catch a dangerous disease or parasite, or be chased and killed by a dog. There are

Every house cat's favorite place: a cushion on a windowsill with a view of the outdoors.

many factors that can threaten a cat's life. If there is a sudden outbreak of disease, such as bird flu or rabies for example, even vaccinated cats should remain indoors.

Good Neighbors

When it comes to neighbors, there are many more issues than you might think. You might live near a cat lover who tries to tempt your cat away from you using lots of daily treats. But there are also the people who may be irritated by your cat because she invites herself into their house, fights with their pet, or eats their pet's food. Then there are the kind of people who cannot stand cats because they go to the bathroom in their child's sandbox or in their flower beds, hunt the fish from the fishpond, leave paw prints on the car roof, or shed all over the garden furniture. These are all good reasons to consider keeping your cat inside, especially if you want to get along with your neighbors.

EXTRA
Cat-Proofing Your Home

See the World Through a Cat's Eyes

A house, apartment, or secure backyard is not without its dangers for your kitten. Just like small children, cats are incredibly curious and will want to explore every nook and cranny, and they cannot tell what is dangerous and what is not. Look around your house or yard. Try to think about what a cat would find interesting and just have to investigate at all costs. Look at your house through the eyes of your cat and eliminate all possible dangers.

Nets

If at all possible, you should make your balcony secure. There are some companies that specialize in making balconies and terraces secure for pets. They should be able to advise you and your parents on the best ways of doing this. Using safety nets, dowels, screws, cable, and clamps, it is relatively easy to put the net up on your balcony. However, if you rent your property, you will need to discuss any changes you want to make to the house with your landlord first.

Safety Check

- [ ] poisonous plants—this includes many well-known and popular horticultural and ornamental plants (also see the list of toxic garden plants)
- [ ] open oven, dishwasher, washing machine, dryer, refrigerator, freezer, and fireplaces
- [ ] draperies and tablecloths hanging down
- [ ] electric cable
- [ ] plastic bags, open garbage cans
- [ ] small parts such as needles, beads, screws, nails, tacks, etc., which could be swallowed
- [ ] household cleaners, disinfectants, tablets and pills, fertilizers, pesticides, and other chemicals
- [ ] open hopper windows
- [ ] tinsel and other holiday decorations
- [ ] slippery floors, glass doors, swinging doors, fragile ornaments
- [ ] hot items: plates, cigarettes, candles, iron
- [ ] unsecured balcony

→ Caution!

Poisonous Garden Plants

anemone
apricot
arnica
arum
autumn crocus
belladonna
boxwood
broom
buttercup
carnation
castor oil plant
catalpa
Christmas rose
cockle
crocus
daffodil
daphne
dogwood
dwarf mistletoe
edelweiss
euonymus

fern
field pansy
field violet
firethorn
geranium
hepatica
Hercules herb
honeysuckle
hyacinth
imperial crown
iris
ivy
jasmine
juniper
laburnum
larkspur
lily of the valley
marsh marigold
mistletoe
monkshood
narcissus

oleander
opium poppy
pasque
primrose
privet
rhubarb
snowball
spurge
stonecrop
tansy
thimble
thuja
tobacco plant
tomato plant
tulip
vetch
wild lupine
wisteria
yew

Poisonous Houseplants

African violet
amaryllis
anthurium
azalea
calla
Christmas cactus
clivia
coral berry
crown of thorns
cyclamen
decorative fern
desert rose
dumb cane
gum
holly
Japanese aralia
orchid
philodendron
poinsettia
pothos

Offer your cat some cat grass before she starts chewing on your other houseplants.

Welcome Home!
The Kitten Moves In

Before your kitten moves in, decide where you are going to place his food and litter box. Cats are creatures of habit and will not adjust very well to things being moved around. Then, once everything is in place and all preparations complete, you are ready to go and pick up your new kitten.

The Right Time

Holidays such as Christmas are not a good time for your new kitten to settle in because everyone is so busy, and you may not have the time or patience required to help your kitten settle in properly and get to know him. Wait a few days until after all the celebrations have passed. After the holidays, the kitten will have more time to adapt to his new environment and get used to all his new people.

Along with the pedigree papers, which should be signed by a reputable breeders club, you should also expect a certificate to show your cat has been vaccinated.

Picking Up Your Kitten

So, at last, the big day has come, and it is time to go and pick up your new kitten. Put him in the pet carrier and leave him be until you get home. No matter how loudly he meows or pleads to be let out of his "prison," do not take him out of his carrier until you are home. Better safe than sorry—you would not want to lose him. Many breeders will start you on your way with some cat litter and also some food that the kitten has previously eaten.

→ No Appetite?

For the first few days, it is quite possible that your kitten may not show any signs of having an appetite due to all the excitement of his new home. You may find yourself worrying that he will starve to death and try to tempt him with a few treats. Warning: Cats love to be pampered, and once you have given him a taste of something special, it might be very difficult to encourage him to eat his normal food. So do not panic, and leave it up to nature. Some cats may be nervous about their new environment and have diarrhea. If this has not settled down after two or three days then you should take your cat to the vet.

Let the Cat Out of the Bag…

When you bring your kitten home, it is best to set the carrier down in the middle of the room so that it is easier for him to come out whenever he is ready. Watch him inspect every inch of his new living quarters. Some kittens will courageously explore their new home, while others are more cautious.

Where to Go to the Bathroom?

After a while, lift the kitten up and put him in his litter box. You may need to do this two or three times. A cat gets used to his new bathroom fairly quickly.

Bon Appétit!

Sooner or later, he will be hungry. Give him whatever he is already used to eating. He will require several small meals a day, so you can simply leave the food out for a few hours (unless the weather is very warm). Cats do not usually overeat. Instead, they eat small portions of food throughout the day.

The First Few Days

These first few days are important for establishing the cat-human bond. You can make your kitten's experiences in his new home very positive, and because cats are such curious creatures, you will soon discover what grabs his interest. Watch him play and stroke and cuddle him, but do not disturb him when he is sleeping or eating.

Holding Your Kitten

Do not pick your kitten up by the scruff of his neck. Put one hand on his body, just behind his front legs, and the other supporting his bottom. You can settle him in the crook of your arm. Kittens like to nestle into this space in your arm.

Everything is new for your kitten. Take the time to feed him, stroke him, and play with him, and he will soon adjust to his new home.

The New Cat Parent

Building a Better Bond With Your Kitten

Spend Plenty of Time at Home

Spend as much time as possible with your new kitten. He will not like to be left alone. He is used to the constant company of his mother and siblings, so you should try to recreate this experience for him by being his new caregiver and playmate.

Your Friends Should Be Patient

It is only natural that your friends are eager to see your new kitten, and that you are excited to show him off. But make sure you wait at least a few days after bringing him home so that he is not completely overwhelmed by lots of people wanting to play with him. He would only end up hiding somewhere and then your friends would not be at all impressed!

Do Not Chase Your Kitten

You should never run after your kitten as this will make him feel scared and then he will try to hide. This is the last thing you want. He may not come out of hiding for a long time and even when he does, he might feel frightened of you.

Simply Sit and Wait

Here is a secret that seems odd, but just give it a try: the less you pick up your kitten and hold him, the more likely he is to climb onto you all by himself, purr on your lap, and fall asleep.

Do Not Boss Him Around

Instead of bossing him around and picking him up constantly, allow him to do his own thing. Simply dangle a toy on a string in front of him and watch him play. If you must pick him up, put one hand on his belly and one under his bottom so that you are supporting him correctly and do not hurt him when you pick him up.

Give Your Kitten a Name

Your new kitten will need a name! Say the name over and over again while you are playing with him, stroking him, or giving him a treat. Use a gentle, loving voice when you say his name. Do not scold him with his new name. He will respond best to a name with two syllables, usually ending in an "ee" sound (Alfie, for example). If the name is too long and complicated, your kitten will not feel as though he is being addressed.

What Your Cat Needs

Sleeping

You may see your kitten creeping up her scratching post into the small plush hammock or bed and give you a saucy look as if to say, "I like this, I think I will sleep here." A cat bed which sits on the ground and may be accessible to your dog, for example, will not be nearly as popular. Of course, there can be exceptions. You may have a friendly dog that your kitten soon comes to adore. The kitten may even opt to climb in the dog's bed with him to keep warm. Cushions on top of shelves are also popular places because they give the kitten a great view of her surroundings.

Eating

Place the food bowls in the kitchen or hallway. The water bowl should be in a different place because cats do not drink in the same place they eat. It is a good idea to put the bowls on a mat that can be easily cleaned because even the most graceful cat is bound to spill her food all over the place!

Shopping List

- [ ] pet carrier
- [ ] 2 food bowls
- [ ] 1 water bowl
- [ ] cat litter
- [ ] scoop
- [ ] scratching post with sleeping area
- [ ] comb
- [ ] brush
- [ ] toys
- [ ] food and treats (the same food the breeder used)

Other items that may be necessary:

- [ ] safety devices/ nets for window, balcony, or backyard
- [ ] cat flap
- [ ] leash and harness
- [ ] mat for bowl
- [ ] disinfectant spray
- [ ] lint roller

Litter Box

Cat litter boxes come in many different designs, and some litters are odor-absorbing or scented. As a rule, a kitten will use any type of litter box, as long as it has litter inside. The litter box should be placed in a quiet corner and made easily accessible at all times.

Playing

Cat toys should be the right size for your cat, such as toy mice, balls, and the like. Buy more than one because they always seem to get lost.

Safe Journey

The pet carrier should be a good size and sturdy. Make sure the door shuts securely and does not loosen over time, the floor is waterproof, and the cat has room to move. Remember that your little kitten will soon grow into an adult cat. For air travel, plastic carriers are a must.

Scratching

Sharpening claws is a necessity for a cat. It is also a sensory pleasure. It is as much a part of her ritual as going to the bathroom, and she also scratches to mark her territory. Because you will not want your cat to damage your sofas or doors with scratch marks, get her a scratching post that is made of a material called sisal. You can also get scratching boards, wall corner protectors for scratching, and much more. The best place to put her scratching post is somewhere between her sleeping and feeding areas.

Grooming

When you buy a cat brush or comb, also buy a lint roller for your rugs, upholstery, and clothes. Short-haired cats only need  to be brushed about once a week. The denser and longer the coat, the more you will need to groom your cat.

Feeding and Caring for Your Kitten

Simply the Right Nutrition
Daily Meals

The wide range of cat food available means it is fairly simple to make sure your cat eats a healthy diet. Many foods are age appropriate and most contain the necessary nutrients for a balanced diet. The easiest way to feed your kitten is to find a ready-made food that is designed specifically for kittens. Feed your kitten at the same time every day so that your kitten quickly learns to come to you for food at the right time.

Food for Juniors

You do not need to be a nutritional expert in cat food ingredients. You can be sure that your kitten will get everything he needs from a good quality food. Trying to put together a balanced diet for your kitten by yourself is no easy task. Particularly while he is growing, your kitten needs small amounts of calcium as well as other vitamins and minerals, which can be found in any good quality complete kitten food.

Favorite Food for Life

The best way to feed your kitten is with canned or dry food. Either type contains a mixture of meat (muscle, heart, liver, and lungs). They also contain a small amount of grain products, such as rice, corn, barley, and wheat, as well as vegetables, vitamins, and minerals. The dry food is made by removing 10 to 15 percent of the water content. Manufacturers offer food in varying quality and price ranges.

If your cat eats mostly dry food, make sure he has plenty of water to drink.

→ How Much to Feed Your Cat

Age of cat (months)	Bodyweight in pounds	Meals per day	Estimated daily amounts in ounces
2–4 months	2.0–3.5	4–5	6.5–10.5
4–5 months	3.5–4.5	3–4	10.0–10.5
5–6 months	4.5–5.5	2–3	8.0–10.0
6–8 months	5.5–7.5	2	8.0–11.5
From 8 months	9.0–10.0	2	10.5–11.5

To choose high quality is never a bad idea. Cats can live long, healthy lives eating the same food day in and day out, but some cats prefer a variety of different foods.

Dry Food

Compared to wet food, dry food has some big advantages. It is more hygienic and can be left out for longer, especially in the summer. You can leave it out all day without worrying about it spoiling or being covered in flies.

Paté or Chunky?

Any good quality food for proper feline nutrition is all very well, as long as your cat actually eats it. But there are many fussy cats who refuse to eat certain types of food. If your cat is ignoring his food, try a different brand or flavor (there are lots of varieties, such as duck, turkey, tuna, etc.). You could also try a different type, such as paté, chunky, with sauce, and other textures. You will soon be able to determine whether your cat was just being fussy or whether he has a genuine eating disorder. Ask your vet if it is okay to add yeast, vitamins, or vegetable flakes to the food for added nutrition. Some cats really like these, so you can sprinkle some into their food on a daily basis. You can also find vitamin-enriched cat food toppings at many pet supply stores.

À la Carte for the Cat?

An alternative way to feed your cat is to cook the food for him yourself. However, by cooking, you could lose a lot of the essential vitamins, not to

mention the amount of trouble you would have to go to. If you decide you want to do this, make sure you read up on the subject. Please bear in mind that preparing meals for your cat from scratch is not always a good idea; for example, liver is rich in vitamins A and D, but too much vitamin A can cause bone overgrowth and even paralysis.

Fresh Meat

From time to time, you could give your cat some fresh meat in addition to his usual diet. Always ask your vet before making any major changes to your cat's diet. Also consider where the fresh meat would come from. Going to your trusted local butcher is safer than picking up meat from the supermarket, which can be full of chemicals and not the cleanest or freshest cut of meat. If your vet gives you the okay, give your cat fairly big chunks so he has to tear the meat and really make use of his teeth. Freshwater fish, chicken, turkey, and raw eggs are frequently infected by salmonella. Some cats go wild for fresh meat, but be aware of the hazards and cook the meat thoroughly. Never feed your cat raw fish or eggs! See the food guide on page 36.

Whatever you decide to feed your kitten, make sure you give him lots of small meals because he has a tiny stomach.

Room Temperature

The food should be room temperature and never given to your kitten directly from the refrigerator. A cat's stomach cannot tolerate food that is too cold, and it will usually be rejected. You can let a can that has already been opened and refrigerated warm to room temperature, or scoop out the food onto a microwave-safe dish and pop it in the microwave for ten seconds.

Every Cat Is Different

Your cat should eat until he is satisfied but not eat so much that he becomes overweight. Look on the packaging of the food to find out how much you should feed your cat based on his weight. Also see page 34 for a rough guide to how much food your cat requires. But besides weight, other factors to consider when deciding how much to feed your cat include activity level, age, breed, metabolism, genes, and health. Every cat is different. Ask your vet to help you figure out how to meet your cat's individual needs.

Slowly and Enjoyable

Unlike dogs, which seem to gobble down every meal as if it is their last, cats take their sweet time eating their food and chew large chunks slowly and with great relish. A cat may run over to his food as if he is starving and then change his mind, only to eat later, so it is best to leave the food out for as long as you can.

A cat will be able to tell whether or not his food is appealing by sniffing it. If it is too cold, the food will not smell appetizing for him and he will probably reject it.

Cats need fresh water. If your cat does not like to drink from a regular bowl, you could try buying a pet fountain. Fresh, running water may entice him to drink more.

Flies and Cat Food

Make sure any wet food you give your cat has not spoiled. In winter, this is not such a huge problem. The food will stay fresh, even if you leave it standing for quite a while. In summer, however, bacteria will grow very quickly on the food and flies will lay eggs in the meat, so do not leave it out for more than an hour. During the day, you can leave out dry food.

Rainwater

A cat can survive a surprisingly long time without food. However, he can only live without water for a few days. When outside, cats prefer to drink from puddles. Some indoor cats like the water from the indoor fountain or rainwater from a plant pot on the balcony, yet they never drink out of their water bowls, possibly because it is chlorinated.

No Milk

Ordinary milk is not good for cats. Many cats get diarrhea from milk and cream because they are lactose intolerant. Lactose is a sugar naturally found in milk. If your cat really enjoys dairy, many pet supply stores sell a special kind of milk that is safe for cats.

Green Stuff for Cats?

Cats nibble on houseplants occasionally or tufts of grass in the yard. Cats use grass as a digestive aid. They do not need to do this on a regular basis, but when there is a gradual buildup of fur, which they swallow when grooming themselves, in their stomach, the hair ball can lead to indigestion.

Grass as a Digestive Aid

Eating grass stimulates a sensitive stomach, which then triggers vomiting. If the cat does not vomit, then the hair ball could cause an obstruction in the intestines or stomach, in the worst-case scenario. Cats who go outdoors do not need a cat grass plant but your indoor cat will need to nibble on cat grass occasionally. You can buy prepackaged seed trays of cat grass from most pet shops, or alternatively, you can buy it in the form of a paste.

This cat has not suddenly turned vegetarian! Cats need grass to help get rid of any fur they swallowed while grooming themselves.

Eyes, Ears, Nose, and Skin
Your Cat's Health

Do the eyes, ears, nose, fur, and bottom all look okay? When you are cuddling your cat, give her a quick once-over to check that everything looks healthy.

Wipe the Eyes

You will only need to do this occasionally for your cat, and it does not require too much fuss. Just use a cotton swab or tissue. Some Persian cats secrete a lot of tears, so you may need to clean their eyes on a daily basis. If the secretion has dried in the corners of the eyes, it is best to use a cotton swab moistened with warm water.

Inside the Ears

Even cats are not capable of cleaning inside their ears. If the ear seems to be too waxy, then look in as far as you can and carefully clean the outer ear with a cotton swab. Never push the cotton swab inside the ear. If you notice a black-brown crust on the ear, this could be a sign of ear mites, so take the cat to see your vet.

Trimming the Claws

Get the vet or someone experienced to show you how to trim the claws. A cat's claws are worn down naturally by jumping, climbing, and playing, but you still might need to cut them. It is best to let your cat sharpen her claws on a scratching post.

Kitty Bath

Most cats will absolutely not tolerate being bathed. Unfortunately, in the case of skin diseases, there is no alternative. Baths are a good idea for Persian cats because this stops their fur from becoming matted so quickly. You should get your Persian cat used to having a bath from a very early age and bathe her on a regular basis. Whether you are giving your cat a bath for medical or aesthetic reasons, you will need someone to help you hold your cat still while you wash her. Put a rubber mat in the bottom of the bath, fill the bath about four inches with warm water, cover her with water from head to tail, and then lather her fur with a special cat shampoo. Be very careful not to get shampoo in her eyes, nose, or ears. Rinse thoroughly, wrap her in a towel, and dry her off. Do not allow her to go outdoors for the rest of the day, and also make sure she keeps warm and out of any drafts.

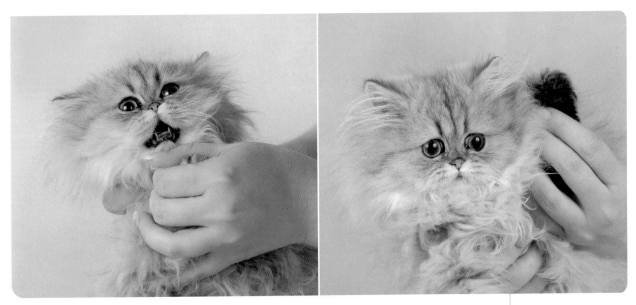

If you have noticed that your cat gets her front claws stuck in the carpet, it is probably time for a manicure. Use a special nail clipper, being careful to avoid the blood vessels called the quick, near the tips of the claws.

Check the Teeth

Gingivitis and plaque buildup are becoming increasingly common. From time to time, check your cat's teeth and gums. Your vet will be able to remove any buildup of plaque.

Cleaning the Bottom

A cat is usually perfectly able to keep her bottom clean. If she has an itchy bottom, she may drag herself along the ground on her bottom or scratch herself. It could be that the anal glands have become clogged or that she has worms. The vet will be able to determine the reason. With Persians, this can sometimes be due to long fur in the way of the anus, which then gets covered in feces when she goes to the bathroom. Let the feces dry and then remove them by combing them out.

If it is heavily soiled, wash the area thoroughly with a mild shampoo and lukewarm water.

Examine the Fur

If your cat always seem to be scratching herself, she may have fleas, mites, lice, or fungus. Examine the fur thoroughly on a regular basis, right down to the skin. If the skin looks inflamed or you find something in the fur that should not be there, for example black specks, crusty flakes, or creepy-crawlies, take your cat to the vet. Any burrs, dirt, or pine needles can be removed with a comb or brush or, if necessary, a bath. If a cat is not used to being combed, she might protest, so be very gentle and use a soft comb. This will feel to her as if she is being stroked. But if she sees you marching toward her with a comb, then she may run away! Find somebody to help you hold her still while you comb her. See the following page for more advice on grooming your cat.

Your cat's ears, eyes, nose, skin, and bottom should be checked on a daily basis. Also check the teeth every now and again for a buildup of plaque. Claws may need trimming if they are too long.

Head-to-Toe Care

Cats are cleaning fanatics and devote much of their time to personal grooming. Healthy kittens start to wash themselves from the age of two to three weeks. When their mother licks them clean, they purr because they enjoy it, which is why your cat purrs when you stroke her.

Prevent Matting

Long-haired cats are not big on being groomed. The dense fur of their undercoat is easily matted and this can be painful when combed. Combing out knots in your cat's fur can cause her to scratch you. Get your kitten used to being groomed from a very early age, and then reward her with small treats and play, which will help her enjoy the grooming experience more. Using force to groom her will make the experience too negative and unpleasant.

Persian Rug—The Daily Battle

The long, thick fur of the Persian cat must be groomed on a daily basis. If you fail to do this, the fur will become hopelessly matted and you will need to cut the knots out with scissors. You will need to use a special steel comb with rounded teeth of different lengths. The fur will need to be combed in layers, starting from the tips and working your way up to the roots.

Hair care is important! Every elegant kitty cat likes to look her best, so make sure you groom her with a comb.

→ *Handy Tip*

Do not forget the chest, abdomen, and insides of the legs. Gently lift your cat up by the front legs to access these areas. Let small amounts of dirt dry, and then use powder and a comb to brush it out. If heavily soiled, wash the area with mild shampoo and lukewarm water in the sink and dry with a towel. If he has a stud tail (unneutered males sometimes secrete excess hormones making the tail greasy and matted), massage flour into the fur, leave it for a while so it soaks up the grease, and then carefully brush it out. You could also try washing the area with a degreasing detergent.

Comb or Brush?

Brushes are not suitable for long-haired cats because they only tidy the fur superficially rather than get out all the tangles. As previously explained, steel combs with blunted teeth are necessary for high-maintenance fur.

Fragrant Powder

Every now and again, you can give your Persian cat a treat by covering his fur in a special scented powder. Spread it into his fur and leave it in overnight. The next day, carefully comb out the powder. So now not only do you have a fragrant-smelling cat, but it will make daily grooming much easier.

Medium-Length Fur

Cats with medium-length fur are relatively easy to groom, however combing still needs to be done on a daily basis. Using a comb with teeth of various lengths, comb out the layers of the top coat and then the undercoat, going from the tips and gradually making your way to the root.

Shorthairs

The daily care of a short-haired cat is not at all time-consuming. He can be easily groomed simply by regular stroking. This gets rid of any fur that has fallen out and encourages blood flow to the skin, which is vital for a healthy, shiny coat. It is a good idea to get a soft brush with rubber studs so that you can brush him when he sheds. This will stop him from swallowing too much fur when he grooms himself.

A Bright Idea

Smooth the fur after combing with a damp cloth to the skin, which causes the fur to lie flat against the body and gives it a beautiful sheen. Always comb and smooth the fur in the direction it grows.

Cats take their grooming very seriously and invest a lot of time in their beauty regimes. Support your kitten in his fight against shedding!

Cats are, by their very nature, not fans of traveling. Take some time to think about how you can care for your cat when you go on vacation.

> *Cats prefer to remain in their own home when you go on vacation. Find someone you can trust to look after your cat because she would really rather stay at home.*

At Home

Cats prefer to remain in familiar surroundings and really will not miss out on traveling all over the place. So this means the best solution is to find someone you trust to look after your cat while you are away. Ask your friend to feed your cat twice a day and clean out the litter box. It would be ideal if your friend could take time to talk to your cat, play a few games, and give her a cuddle, which will help your cat's overall well-being in your absence. Get your friend to come around and get to know your cat before you go away. Do not forget that two cats will not be as lonely as one.

Stay With Friends

Maybe you would prefer to know your cat had constant company while you are on vacation, and she would be okay with leaving her home. In this case, take your cat to your friend's house several times before you go away, so your cat has a chance to get used to it and it will not feel so strange. Do not forget to bring her bowls, cat litter, bed, and toys. And most important of all, ensure you provide her with enough food to last while you are away.

Take Your Cat With You

Another solution is to take your cat on vacation with you, although this would be fairly stressful for her. For vacations in hotels, apartments, or camping, you

should check first whether cats are welcome. Pets need health certificates, which are like pet passports, when they travel. Your cat will need to have certain vaccinations before she is allowed into some countries. Find out the entry requirements of the country you are visiting by checking with your travel agent or vet.

Cat Hotel

Only place your cat in a cat hotel if you really have no other option. For an animal as sensitive as a cat, this arrangement will cause her quite a lot of stress.

Pet Sitter

If you do not have any cat friendly acquaintances, then you could try to seek out a professional pet sitter. Perhaps you have a friend who has used a pet sitter's services or you can look one up in the newspaper or on the Internet.

In the Car   Tip

Whether you decide to take your cat away with you or get a friend to look after her, it is still a good idea to get your kitten used to car journeys while she is still young. Even the occasional visit to the vet will not be so traumatic if your cat is used to traveling in the car.

No Babies, Please
Neutering and Spaying

An unneutered male or unspayed female does not make for a happy cat and is not good for animal welfare. If he or she is kept inside the house, his or her behavior can become quite unbearable both for the animal and the owner alike.

Female: In Heat and Twitchy

A female can get pregnant starting from the age of six to nine months. From spring to early autumn, a healthy cat will be in heat every fourteen days. She will become restless, rolling around on the ground, making cooing sounds, and caterwauling for a mate. The condition lasts several days and will get on everyone's nerves. After three or four of these episodes, any owner would decide enough is enough and get her spayed!

Get your cat neutered if you do not want to breed him. Often, neutering makes the cat more affectionate.

A sexually mature, unneutered male can be quite a handful.

Male: Potent and on the Prowl

A sexually mature male will mark his territory with foul-smelling urine. An advantage of neutering is that it will stop him from roaming and straying away from the house. He will not spend so much time running around outside looking for a mate. Some unneutered males disappear for days or weeks and some never come home again.

What Is Altering?

To prevent all these difficult problems, males and females can be given an operation to make them infertile. For the male, the testes are removed, and for the female, the uterus and ovaries are taken out. The procedure is done under anesthesia and is very quick and easy for a male. He will recover within the same day and soon be running around again. The operation for the female is a little more complicated because it involves an abdominal incision, and she will need a few days to recover.

After Surgery

This is very important. After your cat has been operated on, do not let your other cats near him. The smell of anesthesia is often unpleasant to cats and because his scent will be very strange, his cat buddies may not recognize him and may reject him permanently. Keep other pets away from him until he has completely healed.

Sterilization

You may have heard of female cats being "sterilized" instead of spayed, but this is not the correct term. Sterilization means that the fallopian tubes are disconnected but the ovaries continue to function, still producing hormones and thereby causing the cat to go into heat, even though she cannot actually get pregnant. So this means that although sterilization makes a female cat infertile, it does not prevent the heat cycle and the associated behavior.

The Cat's Character Is Not Affected

Unfortunately, many people believe that their cats will change after being neutered. In fact, unneutered cats who never have the opportunity to find a mate often change their character for the worse. It is also wrong to claim that neutering makes cats fat and lazy. You may only need to reduce his food by a small amount. If you feed him slightly less and play with him more, then you should not notice a problem.

Altered as Early as Possible

It is possible and advisable to get the neutering or spaying done at a fairly early stage, but not until the cat is almost grown (six months for females and eight months for males). In recent years, people are tending to get their cats neutered or spayed quite early and this is not a bad idea because it protects against unwanted pregnancies and also uterine disorders.

A male and female kitten will get along very well as long as both of them have been fixed.

→ Adulthood? You Can Hear and Smell It

Adulthood for a cat is when his skeleton stops growing. You may be able to tell because his appetite will ease off. The female will have her first heat cycle and show that she is sexually mature by giving a loud wailing mewl. She will also display herself by rolling around and showing off her behind. Females have their first heat cycle by the age of six to nine months, which means she is now capable of getting pregnant. Males take a little longer to reach sexual maturity, however gradually their behavior will change. Therefore, you should get your tomcat neutered by nine months of age.

Do not wait until your cat is ill or there is an emergency to introduce her to your vet. It is better to take her there for her first visit quite early on so that she can get used to the process and your vet can answer any questions you may have. You may forget what you need to ask, so make some notes before you go. Your cat will need an annual vaccination, so you could also ask for a general health check for her at the same time.

> When you are in the waiting room at the vet's office, always keep your kitten in a carrier because of the danger of contracting contagious diseases and parasites from other animals.

Straight to the Vet

Do not hesitate to take your cat straight to the vet if you observe the following changes: salivation and panting; dull, scruffy coat; or pasty or liquid defecation. Better to be safe than sorry!

Vaccinations Are Vital

Vaccinations give your cat reliable protection against the most dangerous infections. Vaccines are categorized as either core or noncore. Core vaccines are the ones the American Association of Feline Practitioners (AAFP) believes should be given to all cats: a rabies vaccine and a combination vaccine that includes panleukopenia (FPV), feline herpesvirus (FVR; cat flu), and feline calicivirus (FCV; cat flu). Noncore vaccines are only given to certain cats, depending on their age, breed, health, and risk of exposure to the disease. Examples of noncore vaccines are feline leukemia (FeLV) and feline infectious peritonitis (FIP).

Panleukopenia (FPV)

Panleukopenia, also known as feline distemper, is a highly contagious, feverish disease, and the pathogen is very resistant. However, there has been an effective vaccination against this disease for many years now.

The Cost

As a generous estimate, you may need to set aside about $1,200 a year for your cat. Good quality food, litter, and grooming products are included in this amount, as well as the vaccinations for feline distemper, flu, leukemia, and rabies. You may spend less if you decide to hunt for bargains and use lower quality goods.

Cat Flu (FVR, FCV)

Cat flu is the common name given to a group of viruses, including feline herpesvirus and calicivirus, that cause flulike symptoms in cats. It afflicts cats of all ages. Young cats are particularly

vulnerable. The name plays down the severity of the disease. The treatment of diseased animals is very difficult and may take several weeks for the cat to recover. A vaccination against this is vital.

Noncore Vaccines (FeLV, FIP)

Feline leukemia and feline infectious peritonitis vaccines are recommended only for cats with a risk of exposure to the diseases. Feline leukemia is caused by a virus that not only attacks the various organs but also weakens the cat's immune system. It is only transferred from one cat to another through the saliva. A test can show whether the virus is present in the blood. The vaccination for this needs an annual booster. Feline infectious peritonitis attacks the immune system, and the disease is fatal in most cases. But there are also animals that carry the virus without showing any signs of illness. This vaccination also needs an annual booster.

Rabies

Rabies can affect all mammals, including humans. The rabies virus is one of the most dangerous because it affects the nervous system and the brain, and the incurable symptoms of this disease eventually lead to death. Cats that go outdoors must be vaccinated against rabies. Indoor cats should be, too, in case they manage to escape.

Fleas, Ticks, Worms

All cats must be wormed regularly. Some vets will recommend that both outdoor and indoor cats receive protection from fleas and ticks all year around, not just during the warm seasons. You can get the medication from the vet, which you apply onto the cat's skin at the back of the neck.

Even if your cat bounces out of bed every morning, take her to the vet for an annual checkup so your vet can get to know her and examine her for any potential health problems.

Quick Diagnosis

→ *The Most Common Feline Illnesses*

Symptoms	Possible Causes	Treatment
Vomiting	Gastritis, intestinal obstruction, infectious diseases such as feline immunodeficiency virus (FIV) or feline leukemia	Feed your cat his usual diet. After two days, take him to the vet. If he is vomiting excessively, take him immediately to the vet.
Constipation	Hair balls, foreign bodies, bowel obstruction	If he has not defecated for two days, then take him to the vet.
Diarrhea	Worms, poisoning, infectious diseases (FIV, feline leukemia)	Worm him if necessary. If diarrhea lasts for more than two days, take him to the vet.
Lameness	Insect bite, cut, broken bone, or torn claw	Examine his limbs. An insect bite can be treated with a vinegar–water mixture, but any other problems will need to be addressed by the vet.
Paralysis	Rabies, spinal injury, pelvic fracture	Take him to the vet immediately. If you suspect a pelvic fracture, move your cat as little as possible and transport him in a padded pet carrier.
Convulsions	Poisoning, epilepsy, rabies	If your cat has epilepsy, wrap him gently in a towel so he cannot cause himself any damage and take him to the vet immediately.

Symptoms	Possible Causes	Treatment
Nasal discharge *(watery or bloody)*	Infectious diseases (cat flu, feline infectious peritonitis), foreign body in the nose or lungs, toxoplasmosis, poisoning	If the nasal discharge is only on one side and not watery, this indicates a serious problem there (e.g. foreign bodies). Please take him to the vet. This also applies for suspected poisoning. If the nasal discharge is coming out of both nostrils, you can let him sniff it back up again.
Inflammation of the eye	Foreign body, cat flu, in-grown eyelashes	Allow the vet to examine him so you do not damage his eyes.
Swollen nictitating membrane	Worms, neurological causes	When did you last worm your cat? If only one of the membranes is swollen with other symptoms, you will need to visit an eye specialist.
Excessive salivation	Poisoning, tartar, foreign bodies	Examine his mouth. If he is showing other signs of poisoning, take him to the vet immediately.
Head tilt	Ear infection or foreign body in the ear	This is a serious problem; he will need to be examined by a vet.
Excessive thirst	Diabetes, renal failure	Keep an eye on his water intake and measure how much he actually drinks. Take him to the vet to be examined.

My Care Plan

Daily

Water

Change the water at least once a day, and clean the water bowl to get rid of any bacteria.

Food

Feed your cat at least twice daily (for amount and frequency, see page 34). You may provide her with a bowl of dry food as well so she can snack on it throughout the day.

Litter Box

Cats love clean litter boxes. Therefore, remove the clumps of waste from the litter a couple of times a day.

Playtime

Take time to play with your cat. Offer her a toy or simply put her on your lap for a cuddle.

Health Check

Bright eyes? Dry nose? Clean bottom? Check daily that the fur is glossy, eyes are shiny, and the ears, nose, and buttocks are clean, with no discharge. If necessary, gently remove and clean any secretions.

Long-Haired Cats

Long-haired cats such as Persians will need to be combed daily to prevent the fur from getting matted.

Weekly

Cat Grass

Do not forget your cat grass! Trim it and water it twice a week and replace it if necessary.

Litter Box

At least once a week, remove the cat litter from the tray and scrub the tray with hot water and mild detergent, dry it, and fill it with fresh cat litter at least two inches high.

Grooming

Perfectly Styled and Shiny Coat

Brush your cat's fur gently in the direction of growth, and while you are doing this, examine her teeth and clip her claws if necessary.

Monthly

Sleeping Area

Check your kitten's bed and wash her blankets. If you see dark specks (flea dirt), then get her the appropriate treatment from your vet.

Vaccinations

The first and second vaccinations for your kitten should be done three weeks apart. Then, she will need boosters for protection against panleukopenia, feline herpesvirus, feline calicivirus, and rabies every three years. Your vet may recommend additional vaccines.

Vacation

If you want to travel, think carefully about who could look after your cat while you go away. If you want to take her abroad with you, find out what vaccinations she will need to enter the foreign country and do not forget her health certificate.

Understanding and Playing With Your Kitten

Cats are adaptable enough to enjoy life indoors. A kitten that has only ever experienced living in a small apartment will not know any different.

Little Adventures

If you decide to keep your cat indoors, you should play with her frequently and offer her a few adventures. Even if she cannot hunt real mice, she can still have fun with a toy mouse.

No Mouse in the House

A purely indoor cat will most likely never come across a real live mouse. This means she will miss out on some hunting skills, but this is not a problem. You can ensure your cat still enjoys the thrill of the chase by offering her fun toys to play with.

Learning for Life

A kitten's basic daily routine involves a lot of eating, sleeping, and playing. By playing, she learns the skills she needs for life, so make sure you play lots of games with her that involve stalking, sneaking up on, and catching prey.

Playful for Life

Unlike many animals, cats remain playful well into adulthood and even into old age in some cases. They may not jump around as much as they used to, but they can still show determination and

persistence when playing. This playful behavior is one of the reasons cats are so appealing to humans. Cats seem to stay youthful throughout their lives, and this is probably all down to their playful nature. No matter how old she gets, your cat will always view you as her loving pet parent. So play on!

A Toy Mouse for Kitty

Cats use play to practice their hunting skills by creeping, attacking, jumping, and defending themselves. Any cat game or toy should reflect this, and a mouse is a good choice of toy.

Caution!

Do not let your kitten play with wool or string. She may accidentally swallow the string, and it could become tangled up in her intestines, which would then require surgery.

Every Cat Should Play

Cats are born with a play instinct. A kitten that is not playful is either physically ill or has likely been mentally disturbed in some way. It is normal for a kitten to show a consistent desire to play, and she will be very grateful to be able to play games with you. Some examples of games you can play with your cat can be found on pages 60, 61, 66, and 67.

Half an Hour of Play

Make sure you play with your cat for at least thirty minutes every day. Longer is even better. You will probably find playtime with your cat more entertaining than any soap opera on television. Playing keeps your cat physically fit and mentally balanced and ensures she gets plenty of attention. This will prevent your kitten from misbehaving out of boredom and will help to avoid many accidents in the house. It also strengthens the emotional bond between you.

Keeping Fit

Some cats are naturally greedier than others and will eat all day if there are treats available. It may be fun to feed your cat treats, but too many will cause her to be overweight with all the associated health problems. Make your cat work for her treats by hiding them or getting her to try to take them from you. This will make her work harder for her food rather than just eating from her bowl every time.

Mice are great fun! Especially if they are attached to a piece of string and wiggled around in front of your cat.

Making Friends

Making Friends
Living in Harmony With Other Pets

Fighting like cats and dogs? No way! A cat and dog who live under the same roof can become friends.

Dogs and cats are very different creatures, but they can become very good friends. If your kitten grows up with your dog, he can see him as a buddy and not an enemy. If you want to keep both your pets, it will not do them any harm, but it is best that you introduce them when they are both still young.

Love at First Bite

Will it be love at first sight or will there be problems? You will not know until you try. There are many ways you can help your dog and cat get to know each other if one of them was there first. In principle, it is best if one of them is still a baby. Keep them in separate rooms for a couple of days, and then swap them around so they get used to each other's scent. Next, put them both together and talk soothingly to both animals. Do not leave

them alone together. If they behave, reward them both with a treat. Repeat this process as often as necessary, and you should soon see they are getting used to each other.

Two Adult Animals

If two adult animals meet each other for the first time, this could lead to problems. The biggest problem is the very different body language of a dog and a cat. A dog wags his tail because he is happy, but a cat flicks her tail as a sign of aggression or irritation. If a cat lifts her paw it is a defensive gesture, but if a dog lifts his paw he is being friendly. Cats always run away from animals that are much larger than they are, whereas dogs instinctively chase a fleeing animal because dogs have a strong predatory drive. The one good outcome in this scenario is that a cat can hide in a cupboard or jump up on a shelf, and the dog will not be able to reach her. However, you definitely have to end this type of behavior.

Smaller Pets

If you have any smaller animals, such as fish, birds, or rodents, be very cautious with these pets. Protect them from your cat so that none of your animals come to any harm.

→ Take Heart!
It is often possible for cats to live in peaceful harmony with other pets and accept their new housemates eventually, even if they simply reach a wary truce. So do not worry if you have other pets. If you use caution, have patience, and follow certain rules, your pets can all get along and may even form strong and lasting friendships.

Taboo for Cats

The homes of birds, hamsters, guinea pigs, and other small animals need to be kept safe and out of the cat's reach. Make sure your cat is not able to peer in the cages because the sight of this natural predator will cause smaller pets a lot of stress.

Never Leave Pets Alone Together

Nothing's cuter than the sight of your cat and guinea pig cuddling together. However, in order to be on the safe side, never leave smaller pets alone with your cat, even if they seem to get along very well. This is because a small misunderstanding can awaken your cat's hunting instinct, and your guinea pig or other pet would not stand a chance against your cat.

Cat TV: The Aquarium

Cats love to fish, so make sure your fish tank is out of reach to stop him from being tempted. Many cats will sit hypnotized in front of a fish tank for hours, watching it as if it were a television!

This cat has just met a rat for the first time. He has no clue what to make of this strange new creature.

First, he sniffs the rat and the rat becomes very wary.

The cat is getting closer and lifts up a paw to swipe the rat. Not such a great game for the rat!

The Family Cat

Not everyone gets along with everyone else. But animals that share a home must at least learn to tolerate one another, accept each other, and not fight. Some cats will consistently go out of their way to avoid people they do not like. This is usually because they have had a bad experience with this person.

Ideal Home

Choose a cat that you think everyone in the family will get along with. Some older cats are less tolerant, so if you have a large family, it is best to get a young kitten.

→ Do Not Nag

Try to trust your younger sibling with your new kitten, and do not constantly yell at him if he does something wrong. Otherwise, he may lose interest in playing with the kitten.

Cats and Small Children

When small children and cats grow up together, they can get to know each other really well and soon become great friends. Make sure your younger sibling realizes the cat is not a toy, but a playmate and friend who he or she can trust with all his or her secrets. You or a parent should supervise toddlers with cats as toddlers sometimes tend to grab at cats, which could cause the cat to scratch. Do not leave your cat alone with a baby or toddler.

Bad Experiences

Very often, young children may play too roughly with a cat and cause him unintentional pain or aggravation. So consider this: does your younger sibling get along with your cat? If not, explain to him or her that a cat is not like a person who will forgive you if you hurt him, and in the worst case, he may develop a permanent fear of your little brother or sister.

Kittens and small children can become great friends. Show your younger siblings the correct way to play with your kitten.

Never Hit Your Cat!

Even older children and adults sometimes lose the trust of their cats, whether unintentionally or not. If your cat misbehaves, never use physical violence to correct him. It will not work. A cat will not understand being punished for something he did wrong. It is better to reward him when he does something right. This way, the good behavior will occur more frequently while the bad behavior will happen less often or stop.

Rejection Runs Deep

Because of bad experiences, cats can not only develop a fear of a particular person, but they can also fear people with similar characteristics, such as men in general, or people with beards, or someone who wears red trousers, a purple shirt, or stripy socks! The cat has learned to associate a visual cue with pain or fear. This fear can begin from between the third and eighth week of life during the developmental phase. Any bad experience will be permanently burned into his memory. If your cat has any particular fears, you may want to ask your vet about them. If the fears are quite mild, you can try using treats to help him overcome any problems.

The Quickest Way to a Cat's Heart . . .

The person who feeds the cat will create a strong bond with him, so use this to your advantage. If the cat is fearful of a certain person, get him or her to feed the cat some treats. He or she should offer the treats carefully and gently to the cat. The cat may be unsure at first, but eventually greed will win out and with any luck, these two can become friends.

By being kind, you will quickly win the trust of your cat. Cats cannot stand any sudden loud noises and will go out of their way to avoid them.

When Should Your Little Brother or Sister Help Out?

Cats are not really ideal for children under six because they tend to scream loudly and make clumsy, sudden movements, which cats hate. But a little playtime, and showing your younger sibling how to feed the cat, can give him or her a bit of responsibility. You or a parent should always watch the young children of the house when they interact with your cat.

From School-Age Onwards

Once your little brother or sister is old enough to go to school, he or she should learn how to treat a cat gently. This means your younger sibling is ready to take on some new tasks, such as playing with the cat, combing him, or helping to clean out his litter box. Help your little brother or sister with these duties so you can keep a close eye on how things go.

FUN TIPS

Cuddling and Playing
Make Your Cat Your New Best Friend!

Cats Love to Play

Kittens love to play. Do not disturb them when they are sleeping, eating, or using the litter box. When all these activities are finished, then playing will be the only thing on your kitten's mind. He will love dangling toys that he can swipe and catch. He also loves hiding in boxes and pouncing. Kittens are curious and will poke their noses into everything. Observe and see what he likes best. Perhaps he would like to investigate your room?

Safe Toys

There are loads of cat-safe toys you can use to play with your cat, such as wooden or plastic balls, Ping-Pong balls, feather wands, and windup mice. If the toy becomes damaged, throw it out and buy a new one.

Dangerous Toys

Never allow a toy or piece of string to get caught around your kitten's neck. He may suddenly back away in fear and get strangled by the string.

Put Your Toys Away

Do not allow your cat to play with any dangerous objects, such as anything sharp, or things that dissolve, get tangled, or can be easily swallowed. Most important, any sewing items such as needles can be fatal for a cat. Make sure you put very small toys away. Stuffed toys, however, are perfect for a cat to play with. Just make sure your cat does not eat the stuffing!

Boxes Are the Best!

An easy way to keep things interesting is to get some old boxes for your cat to explore and place some food or toys inside. Make sure the kitten can easily climb in and out of the box (open both ends) so that he does not get scared.

No Plastic Bags, Please

Clear all plastic bags away. They are extremely dangerous and definitely not suitable for any games because a curious kitten could easily crawl into one and suffocate. Fabric bags are less dangerous but should not be used as toys.

What Your Kitten Dislikes:

→ being dressed up like a doll
→ baths (unless he gets used to it from a very young age)
→ being locked in a closet
→ getting trapped in a room
→ being pulled around by the tail

What Your Kitten Likes:

→ playing
→ cuddling
→ sleeping in your bed
→ crawling under your blanket
→ playing with your toes
→ looking out the window
→ treats
→ you

Rules of Play

1. Choose a toy, such as a toy mouse.
2. Dangle it in front of your cat but do not hit him with it.
3. Only play the game if your cat is having fun.
4. If your cat scratches you, stop playing immediately.
5. Give him a treat if he plays nicely with you.

What Does "Meow" Mean?
Cat Talk

Animals that would rather stay out of each other's way have no need to talk to one another. They will only communicate with one another if they absolutely have to. A cat can learn a lot about another cat from her scent markings, even if that cat is long gone from the area. Body language also serves as a form of communication and is a sort of private language between cats, just as it is between humans.

Cats communicate with one another using scent and body language, so your cat can get to know the neighbor's cat without having to get too close.

Silent Observer

Just like humans, cats can be real chatterboxes when they want to be. Kittens learn by watching their mother and soon learn that it is rather effective to sit in front of their food bowl and meow when you are looking at them.

Cat Fight!

Cats can often have a lot to say to one another if they are close friends and seem to understand what the other is saying. You may have heard a mother cat talk to her kittens. Cats are very noisy when fighting and can disrupt a whole street in the middle of the night. Also, when cats mate, they make an awful lot of noise. In normal everyday life, cats do not really feel the need to talk but some breeds, such as the Siamese, can be very vocal.

Tummy Rumbles

Perhaps not surprisingly, all cats are talkative when they want something. A reasonably clever little kitten will soon figure out how to meow as pitifully as she possibly can so that everyone in the family rushes to the kitchen to feed her!

Reasons to Meow

Any cat can produce a meow command that says "feed me!" A cat will use different tones when she meows or a particular meow that you as the owner will come to recognize. You may soon be able to distinguish the more urgent meows from the casual chatty ones. All cats have their own individual ways of communicating with their humans.

Shouting and Noise

Dr. Michael W. Fox, a veterinarian and professor, has managed to identify sixteen different sounds made by cats, which fall into three different categories: muttering, singing, and high-pitched noises. Cats have the ability to make all of these noises from the age of twelve weeks, even though their battle cries may not yet be taken seriously by another cat.

Scent-Speak

There have been many books written on the subject of cat language. Several Web sites also provide information on cat communication. Cats use scent and body language far more than any sounds. You can check out your local library or the Internet for specific information on how cats communicate with their humans and other animals.

The Big Stink

Strong-smelling substances such as perfume are too harsh for a cat's nose. These sorts of smells are very unpleasant to a cat.

Cats are very talkative with their humans. They are especially good at the meow that means "feed me!"

Purring

Everyone has heard a cat purr, and many people are well aware of the relaxing effect it has on them. But cats do not just purr when they are feeling content. They also purr if they are injured or feel threatened in some way. It is suggested that cats do this to calm themselves.

Smells Give It Away

Cats always know if you have been stroking another cat or even a dog. Some odors have a strong effect on cats, such as pheromones, which are chemicals given off by animals that trigger a specific response from other members of the same species. Catnip is another substance that cats respond strongly to. It can cause some cats to act crazy.

7 Tips for Training Your Cat

Training for Individuals

Cats are individuals and therefore cannot be trained in the same way you would train a dog. They tend not to follow orders but can learn certain rules, as long as these are kept simple. Cats like to do their own thing! But this is probably one of the reasons us humans admire them so much. Nevertheless, even cats have to learn what is allowed and what is not. With a little patience and a bit of play, you should be able to teach your kitten right and wrong. This will strengthen your kitten's bond with you, and you will have a better behaved adult cat.

Am I allowed to do this or not? If you do not want your cat to shred tissues, teach him this right from the start.

1. Have Patience

The most important requirement for successful training is patience. It may take days before you have a breakthrough, and this can be quite frustrating for you at first. But remember that your kitten is still very young and inexperienced and does not know his family very well yet. Just keep trying!

2. Be Consistent

Be consistent. If you do not allow something the first time, make sure you do not allow him to do it the next day or any other day. For example, if you ban your cat from sitting on the table, and then let him do it the next day, then your rules will not work.

3. Use a Firm Voice

The best means of training a cat is by using a firm voice. Cats respond particularly well to voices, so take advantage of this when training him. A strong "no" spoken loudly and forcefully will be enough to stop your kitten from climbing the curtains or scratching the furniture. When you see him scratching, carry him to his scratching post so he knows where he is able to scratch. Then praise him with quiet, soothing words and a treat. He will soon learn what he is and is not supposed to do.

4. Clap Your Hands

You can enhance the effect of your voice with a clap of your hands, or if he is very disobedient, a water spray. If your kittens are fighting, interrupt this by slamming the door—the noise will startle them into stopping what they are doing.

5. No Physical Punishment

Under no circumstances should you ever punish your kitten by using physical force because this will make him scared of you. This will harm your relationship with your cat and in the worst case, he will never trust you again.

6. Always Use Praise and Love

Praise your cat whenever he behaves. For example, if he scratches on the scratching post, praise him and show him that you are happy.

7. Compromise

If your cat is doing something you are not particularly happy about, decide on whether this really matters. For example, if your cat is happy sleeping on the windowsill, then remove all houseplants and set up a little bed there. You may not like it much, but if he seems to love it, then try to compromise. And is it really so bad if you have to move the plants around to keep him happy?

Praise your kitten if he does something good, such as climbing up his cat tree instead of up your curtains.

Cat Tricks

Teach your cat to do practical things just for the fun of it, such as walking on a leash or traveling in the car with you.

Ever since cat owners realized that cats can be trained, there are a growing number of people who attempt to train their cats. This can be very difficult because many cats do what they like, but it is possible to bribe a cat into doing tricks for you. However, your commands may fall on deaf ears, so make sure you have some very tasty treats and then her hearing will not be quite so selective!

Tricks Are Not Chores

The trick to training a cat is to make her realize that training is not a chore. Your cat is far more likely to learn to do something that she enjoys. For example, you could teach her to go around an obstacle course. It will not take much to distract her from training though, so you may have difficulty getting her to show off her tricks to other people. She will not do it in front of an audience! These stubborn

yet clever animals are more than capable of fishing a toy out of a box which only has a tiny hole at the top. Some clever cats can learn to pull covers off boxes.

Hurdles

Use a piece of string to create a miniature hurdle and allow her to investigate. If she jumps over the hurdle, then give her a treat, for example, a piece of dry food. At the same time shout "jump" or another word. Practice this for a few minutes every day before feeding her. If she gets really good at it, you can try it without the string and get her to jump in the air. A smart cat will soon learn that if she jumps, there is a treat in it for her. You could also try getting her to run through a small tunnel by rolling a ball through the tunnel so that she chases it.

Treats in Boxes

A cat can also learn to fish out treats from a box with small holes in the top. Get a shoe box or something similar, and cut holes the size of ping-pong balls in it. Put some treats in the box and present it to your cat to play with. It will not take her long to figure out what she has to do. You could also put toys or catnip in the box and make the holes a bit bigger so she can fish them out.

No Claws Allowed

Some cats get very carried away during training and may dig their claws in to an outstretched hand or foot. If this happens, immediately stop all play. Look out for fur standing up on the back of the neck, twitching tail, pinned back ears, or a tense body. If you notice any of these signs then look out!

Enough Is Enough

If a cat has had enough, she will either scratch you or walk away. If this is the case then stop training her and leave her in peace.

If you are patient and offer your cat treats, she can do well in her training sessions.

Just for Fun

You should only teach your cat tricks for fun. She will not perform in front of an audience. Do not punish her if she cannot do the tricks. Do not show impatience or frustration or your cat will simply walk away. Keep it fun and simple so that she enjoys herself.

Understand and Be Understood

Cats and Dogs

Friends Forever?

Dogs and cats can get along quite well as long as they have enough time to get used to each other. It will be much easier for them to get along if they grow up together.

Room Swap

Do not just put a cat and a dog in the same room together the first time they meet. This might lead to a fight. Instead keep your cat in one room and your dog in another, and then after a couple of days, get them to swap rooms. This way they will get used to each other's scent.

First Meeting

Now let the dog and cat meet. Praise and reward both animals if they behave well. Repeat this several times.

Good Friends

After several meetings, the animals will most likely be a bit more relaxed with each other. With any luck, they may soon eat together or sleep in the same place.

Training Checklist

- [ ] **Never hit your cat or use force.**
- [ ] **Give him plenty of praise.**
- [ ] **Try to meet his needs.**
- [ ] **Be patient and stay calm.**
- [ ] **Act consistently with clear boundaries.**
- [ ] **Speak clearly and firmly.**
- [ ] **Use gentle training aids such as a water spray.**

Rules of Play

The Perfect Toy

A toy that is small and can be moved around easily is just right. A toy mouse or toy fishing rod is ideal. A ball of wool is not a good idea because your cat may get tangled up in it or eat the string.

Interest in Play

Only play with your cat when she is in the mood. If she wants to eat or sleep then leave her in peace.

Catch the Prey

Mice run away from cats, so try to imitate this with a toy mouse and encourage your cat to give chase.

No Scratching!

If your cat scratches or attacks your hands, then stop playing immediately. But if she behaves well then make sure you praise her.

Mini Cat Dictionary

"Meow" can mean "Open the door!" or "Give me food!"

"Mi-mi" is a friendly greeting. Your cat may make this noise when she wakes you up!

"Murr" says the cat when she is unexpectedly petted. You can take this as an invitation to continue.

A mewl that sounds like a moan is heard when the cat has either brought in a live mouse, or she is in heat.

Scientists have classified cat talk into singing, murmuring, and high-pitched noises.

Singing includes all types of meow noises that a cat makes.

Murmuring includes any noise that the cat makes with her mouth closed, e.g., purring.

High-pitched noises include hissing and growling.

A cat will also make a chattering noise when her prey is out of reach. It is thought she makes this noise because she is frustrated.

Translated from the German edition by Claire Mullen.

Edited and produced by Enslow Publishers, Inc.

Originally published in German.

© 2007 Franckh-Kosmos Verlags-GmbH & Co. KG,
    Stuttgart, Germany
    Hannelore Grimm, *Kätzchen*

Library of Congress Cataloging-in-Publication Data

Grimm, Hannelore, 1947–
  [Kätzchen. English]
  Kittens : keeping and caring for your pet/ Hannelore Grimm.
    pages cm. — (Keeping and caring for your pet)
  Includes bibliographical references and index.
  Summary: "Discusses how to choose and care for a kitten, including diet, behaviors, housing, grooming, exercise, popular breeds, and vet care"—Provided by publisher.
  ISBN 978-0-7660-4186-8
  1. Kittens—Juvenile literature. I. Title.
  SF445.7.G75 2013
  636.8'07—dc23

               2012038633

Paperback ISBN 978-1-4644-0303-3

Printed in the United States of America

052013 Lake Book Manufacturing, Inc., Melrose Park, IL

10 9 8 7 6 5 4 3 2 1

To Our Readers: We have done our best to make sure all Internet addresses in this book were active and appropriate when we went to press. However, the author and publisher have no control over and assume no liability for the material available on those Internet sites or on other Web sites they may link to. Any comments or suggestions can be sent by e-mail to comments@enslow.com or to the address on the back cover.

Every effort has been made to locate all copyright holders of material used in this book. If any errors or omissions have occurred, corrections will be made in future editions of this book.

♻ Enslow Publishers, Inc., is committed to printing our books on recycled paper. The paper in every book contains 10% to 30% post-consumer waste (PCW). The cover board on the outside of each book contains 100% PCW. Our goal is to do our part to help young people and the environment too!

Photo Credits: Color photos taken by Ulrike Schanz especially for the purposes of this book except Juniors Bildarchiv, pp. 15, 18 (middle and bottom), 19; Shutterstock.com, p. 1.

Cover Photo: *Main photo:* Svetlana Markelova/Photos.com (gray and white domestic longhair). *Bottom, left to right:* Shutterstock.com (seal point ragdoll); Marc Jelle Leidekker/Photos.com (gray tabby domestic shorthair); Shutterstock.com (cream Persian, blue domestic shorthair). *Back:* Ulrike Schanz (author photo); Shutterstock.com (white and gray domestic shorthair).

Index

Further Reading

Books

Arden, Darlene. *The Complete Cat's Meow: Everything You Need to Know About Caring for Your Cat.* Hoboken, N.J.: Howell Book House, 2011.

Fogle, Bruce. *Complete Cat Care: What Every Cat Owner Needs to Know.* London: Mitchell Beazley, 2011.

Lee, Justine. *It's a Cat's World . . . You Just Live in It: Everything You Ever Wanted to Know About Your Furry Feline.* New York: Three Rivers Press, 2008.

Internet Addresses

ASPCA: Cat Care
http://www.aspca.org/Home/Pet-care/cat-care

Animal Planet: Pets 101: Cats
http://animal.discovery.com/pets/cats.htm

The Cat Fanciers' Association
http://www.cfainc.org